Gülen on Dialogue

By Frances Sleap & Omer Sener
Edited by Paul Weller

London-based, the Centre for Hizmet Studies provides access to reliable information and resources for serious study of the Hizmet movement. The Centre aims to facilitate, as well as present, critical analysis of Hizmet for both academic and popular audiences. Its activities include research, resource development, online support, discussion forums and print publication.

Gülen on Dialogue

This booklet was originally published by the Dialogue Society in 2013 as a chapter in *Dialogue Theories* by Frances Sleap and Omer Sener. Reprinted here with kind permission of the Dialogue Society.

www.HizmetStudies.org

© Centre for Hizmet Studies 2014

www.HizmetStudies.org
info@hizmetstudies.org

ISBN 978-0-9929312-0-9

Contents

Authors' Acknowledgements

We, the authors of this publication, would like to express our heartfelt thanks to our editor Professor Paul Weller for his invaluable advice, support and belief in the project. We appreciatively acknowledge Ahmet Kurucan's assistance in providing us with his personal lecture notes on Fethullah Gülen's talks on dialogue and Ozcan Keles's valuable input on this publication.

Foreword

This booklet is about the thought and practice espoused and practised by Fethullah Gülen and the Hizmet movement. Fethullah Gülen is one of the most important Muslim scholars of our time for whom dialogue is not just about overcoming problems of our globalising world but is necessitated by our very humanity and his Islamic faith. Therefore, dialogue is an ever-present and underlying theme for Gülen in addition to being a particular area of thought and practice that he seeks to promote and develop. What is significant about Gülen, however, is that he is not just a scholar and thinker but also a doer who has inspired millions to think and act alongside him in what has now emerged as a civil society movement known as the Hizmet movement.

Another reason for Gülen's significance is pointed out by Paul Weller, Professor of Inter-Religious Relations at the University of Derby and Visiting Fellow at Oxford University, who dedicated his book *A Mirror for our Times* (Continuum 2009) to Fethullah Gülen, saying: 'Gülen does not teach a "liberal" or "modernist" version of Islam. Rather, his teaching offers a robust renewal of Islam that is engaged with the contemporary world. It is rooted in a deep knowledge of authentically Islamic sources.' The fact that Gülen bases his ideas and thought (and by extension, the movement its practice) on authentically Islamic sources is significant at a number of levels – not least because it demonstrates how Muslims can engage and respond to modern ideas, culture and society while remaining true to their identity.

Given the importance of dialogue for both Gülen and Hizmet, it is fitting that our first publication as the Centre for Hizmet Studies should be on this subject. This booklet provides a short biography of Gülen's life in relation to his dialogue efforts and then goes on to study the main features and characteristics of his dialogue thought such as: love, tolerance, empathetic acceptance, positive action, and humility. It then explores how Gülen's notion of dialogue, dialogically developed and practised by the Hizmet movement, is now being put into practice in different parts of the world. The section on practice concludes with a list of the twelve 'dialogue principles' developed by UK registered charity the Dialogue Society from Gülen's teachings and the Hizmet movement's practice.

Gülen on Dialogue was originally published as a chapter in *Dialogue Theories* (London: Dialogue Society, 2013), by the same authors, in which ten dialogue thinkers were introduced in the format indicated in the paragraph above. I would highly recommend that book to anyone interested in dialogue and to those interested in Gülen's understanding and practice of dialogue – as it is better appreciated and contextualised in conjunction with other dialogue thinkers and ideas.

In hope that this booklet will inspire deeper discussion and analysis of Hizmet and Gülen, the foci of study for the Centre for Hizmet Studies,

Dr Ismail Mesut Sezgin
Director & Research Fellow

Centre for Hizmet Studies
London, May 2014

Summary

• For Gülen, dialogue is a part of the fabric of Islam, embedded in its very foundation. It is a religious duty, not just encouraged but required by the values and commands of the Qur'an and Sunnah and by the basic character of our God-given human nature. Gülen advocates dialogue because of Islam, not despite it, and not on transient political grounds.

• Gülen sees dialogue as a dynamic process which must be allowed to develop naturally, including as wide a group of people as possible; thus it should be open-ended and inclusive. Dialogue initiatives should move beyond mere words and mutual well wishing to undertakings that bring about real, substantial, meaningful encounters.

• A key point to note about Gülen's approach is that it is based on a human-centric discourse. An important element of Gülen's human-centric discourse is the belief that diversity is intended.

• For Gülen, diversity of race, religion, nation and life-way was intended by God and should be accepted and valued as a route to understanding. Diversity requires us to learn how to live together, which in turn necessitates dialogue. According to Gülen the response to diversity through positive engagement and dialogue is one of the major goals that the divine will has set for humankind.

- Key characteristics to Gülen's dialogue include concepts and teachings such as being a person of the heart *('gönül insanı')*, compassion, humility, empathic acceptance, ability to engage and learn from one another, positive action *(müsbet hareket)* and positive thinking about others *(hüsnüzan)*.

- Through his teachings and sermons, Fethullah Gülen has inspired a transnational civil society movement engaging in education and dialogue, contributing towards more positive relations between groups of different faiths, cultures and political positions. Gülen inspired dialogue charities worldwide undertake tens of thousands of dialogue initiatives and projects each year, trying to reach out to the disengaged.

- In regions affected by ongoing or recent conflict, including Afghanistan, Pakistan, the Philippines, Bosnia-Herzegovina, southeast Turkey and northern Iraq, Gülen-inspired schools welcome students from diverse backgrounds playing an important role in easing inter-group tensions.

- Many people involved in or familiar with the movement inspired by Gülen consider that his teachings and advocacy have attuned a large mass of people to a dialogical outlook in their general approach to interpersonal and inter-group relations.

Biographical Introduction

Muhammed Fethullah Gülen is a Turkish Muslim scholar, opinion leader and peace advocate. He is one of the world's most influential Muslim teachers, the inspiration behind a major transnational civil society movement. He was born in 1941 in the village of Korucuk, in the Erzurum province of Turkey. Between 1959 and 1981 he was a state licensed preacher. During this time and after retiring from this post Gülen travelled extensively in Turkey and abroad, addressing diverse gatherings on issues relating to faith, responsibility, modernity, science and society.

As an Islamic scholar and public intellectual, Gülen has authored over 60 books and continues to write the editorial for a number of periodicals such as *The Fountain,* a magazine of spiritual and scientific thought. His extensive learning in both religious and non-religious disciplines allows him to reach a diverse audience and to bridge-build between disparate fields. One of his on-going intellectual projects is the *Key Concepts of Sufism*, a multi-volume collection of essays explaining how Sufi concepts originate from and are rooted in the Qur'an and Sunnah.[1] He is not a 'liberal', 'modernist' or 'reformer'; he speaks from within the Sunni Hanafi tradition of Islam, offering an authentic re-reading of religion, suggesting new ways of engaging with contemporary ideas and realities. He is widely known for his pro-dialogue and

---

1   The Sunnah consists of the example, instructions and actions of the Prophet Muhammed.

pro-democracy stance, and his utter opposition to any form of terrorism.

Gülen, who topped the July 2008 Foreign Policy and Prospect magazines' poll of most influential public intellectuals, has initiated and inspired a worldwide civil society movement known by participants as Hizmet, literally 'Service', though sometimes referred to as the Gülen Movement, a term of which Gülen disapproves. Participants invest and engage in nondenominational education and intercultural dialogue projects intended to contribute towards durable peace and greater understanding. Loosely connected by shared ideals and principles, the movement is now active across the world through schools, universities, dialogue organisations and other charitable NGOs. Gülen has developed a broad readership and the movement now attracts participants from diverse backgrounds, including people of other religious faiths and none.

While Gülen's exposition of Islam has always been inclusive and dialogic, it was in the early 1990s that he began particularly advocating the need for dialogue initiatives and organisations to ensure that the focus on dialogue continued throughout the year. He set an example by his visits to religious and ethnic leaders such as the Patriarch of the Turkish Orthodox community, the Patriarch of the Turkish Armenian community, the Chief Rabbi of the Turkish Jewish community, leaders of the Turkish Alevi community, Pope John Paul II and the Chief Sephardic Rabbi of Israel. Given his public standing in Turkey, these meetings helped legitimise minority communities among the wider Turkish public. Gülen was personally involved in setting up the Journalists and Writers Foundation, which continues to organise dialogue events bringing together people of opposing viewpoints and divergent lifestyles. These initiatives had a significant, nationwide impact in Turkey with reactions documented in the newspaper columns of the time.

In 2010 Gülen was awarded an honorary doctorate by Leeds Metropolitan University for his contribution to education, peace-making and intercultural dialogue. In 2011 in New York he was awarded an EWI Peace Building Award by the East West Institute for his contribution to world peace. In the same year the Senate of the US State of Texas passed a resolution commending him for his contributions to the promotion of global peace and understanding. Several university chairs have been established to study his work, the most recent being the Fethullah Gülen Chair for Intercultural Studies at the Catholic University of Leuven, Belgium.

Dialogue in Theory

Gülen's conception and practice of dialogue developed through the 1970s and 80s, in the context of modern Turkey where various groups, differentiated by economic class, ideology or kind or degree of religious belonging, confronted each other in latent or open hostility. They shared a language, a land, a long history, yet they were unable to imagine any community of ideas or purposes. Gülen began to address this problem in his role as a state-licensed preacher, preaching not only in mosques but also coffee houses and other public places.

In the early 1990s Gülen encouraged those inspired by his teachings to organise dialogue events and to form dialogue organisations to sustain the momentum of such work. He sought to build bridges between people of different religions, worldviews and backgrounds. Through his teachings and advice he sought to bridge the divide between science and religion, secular and religious worldviews,[2] leftists and rightists, Alevis and Sunnis and Turks and Kurds.[3] He used the arguments and idioms of religion and science to demonstrate the compatibility

---

2   Louis J. Cantori, 'Fethullah Gülen: Kemalist and Islamic Republicanism and the Turkish Democratic Future,' in *Muslim World in Transition: Contributions of the Gülen Movement: Conference Proceedings*, ed. Ihsan Yilmaz et al. (London: Leeds Metropolitan University Press, 2007), 99.

3   Robert A Hunt and Yuksel A. Aslandogan. *Muslim Citizens of the Globalized World: Contributions of the Gülen Movement* (Somerset, N.J.: The Light, 2007), 57.

and indeed interdependence of the two, undermining the
traditional dogmas on both sides which prevented people from
meeting on common ground and developing a shared language.[4]

The kinds of dialogue efforts encouraged by Gülen are inclusive,
open-ended and action-orientated, involve 'ordinary' people and
lead to greater understanding. Gülen sees dialogue as a dynamic
process which must be allowed to develop naturally,[5] including as
wide a group of people as possible; thus it should be open-ended
and inclusive.[6] For Gülen, dialogue itself consists not of dialogue
events but of the interactions that occur as a result of such
occasions. Those interactions must be allowed to develop and
flourish, aided as appropriate by meetings, discussions and other
projects. Dialogue initiatives should be 'action-orientated'[7] in the
sense of moving beyond mere words and mutual well wishing
to undertakings that bring about real, substantial, meaningful

---

4   Fethullah Gülen, 'Science and Religion,' in Knowledge and Responsibility:
     Islamic Perspectives on Science, ed. Ali Ünal (Somerset, NJ: Tughra Books,
     2007).

5   'Diyalog hizmetlerinde herşeyi baştan belirleyemezsiniz. Bazı şeyler vardır
     ki onları ancak ihtiyaçlar ve zaruretler belirler. Bu sistem statik değil sürekli
     hareket halinde olan ve kendini yenileyen dinamik bir sistemdir.' [trans: 'In
     dialogue, you cannot predetermine everything from the beginning. Some
     things can only be determined by needs and necessities. Therefore, dialogue
     is not a static system; it is in constant motion and is a self-renewing dynamic
     system.'] Fethullah Gülen, 'Ikindi Sohbetleri' (Ahmet Kurucan lecture
     notes, Pennsylvania, 16th March, 2006).

6   Fethullah Gülen, Criteria or Lights on the Way, 2nd ed, (Izmir: Kaynak,
     1998), vol. 1, 19.

7   Fethullah Gülen, Toward a Global Civilization of Love & Tolerance
     (Somerset, N.J.: Light, Inc, 2006), 50.

encounters.[8] Dialogue initiatives should engage the grass roots of society rather than only scholars or leaders.[9][10] Finally, dialogue efforts should build mutual awareness and understanding.[11]

Gülen acknowledges that achieving grass root dialogue between ordinary people en masse will take a number of generations owing to entrenched prejudices. However, he states that the present generation must strive to do all it can to eradicate barriers and prejudices between people, helping to lay the foundations for

8   'Diyalog adına kuru söylemlere değil, harekete ihtiyaç var.' [trans: 'In dialogue, we do not need empty rhetoric; what we need is action.'] Fethullah Gülen, 'Ikindi Sohbetleri' (Ahmet Kurucan lecture notes, Pennsylvania, 21st November, 2008).

9   Fethullah Gülen, Toward a Global Civilization of Love & Tolerance, 77; 'Diyalog'da önemli olan halkların halkla buluşmasıdır. Kalıcı ve başarılı olan diyalog ancak budur ve bu yolla gerçekleşir.' [trans: 'What is important in dialogue is for the grass roots/ordinary people ('halk') to meet with one another. Long-lasting and successful dialogue is only this and can only be achieved this way.'] Fethullah Gülen, 'Ikindi Sohbetleri' (Ahmet Kurucan lecture notes, Pennsylvania, 23rd February, 2009). 'Çünkü esas olan taban kitlenin kendi arasında yaptığı diyalogdur. Kalıcı olan budur.' [trans: 'Because what matters is the dialogue that takes place between the grass roots of society. This is what will endure.'] Fethullah Gülen, 'Ikindi Sohbetleri' (Ahmet Kurucan lecture notes, Pennsylvania, 6th April, 2009).

10   While Gülen states that dialogue should reach, include and rest upon the grass roots of society he is not claiming that everyone has an obligation to engage actively in dialogue.

11   Based on Gülen's inclusive understanding of dialogue, the Dialogue Society, a Gülen inspired organisation, defines dialogue as: 'meaningful interaction and exchange between people (often of different social, cultural, political, religious or professional groups) who come together through various kinds of conversations or activities with a view to increased understanding.' 'Our Approach,' Dialogue Society, accessed 25th March, 2013, http://www.dialoguesociety.org/about-us/our-approach.html.

real dialogue en masse in future generations.[12]

Gülen's understanding of dialogue is not based on pragmatism; it is not a strategy to limit the threat posed by competing groups. Rather, it is deeply rooted in Islamic sources, such as the Qur'an, the Sunnah, *tasawwuf* (Sufism),[13] as well as nature, history, and contemporary perspectives. For Gülen, dialogue is a part of the fabric of Islam, embedded in its very foundation. It is a religious duty, not just encouraged but required by the values and commands of the Qur'an and Sunnah and by the basic character of our God-given human nature. Gülen advocates dialogue because of Islam, not despite it, and not on transient political grounds. Since Gülen's thought on dialogue is grounded in theology, it is possible to refer to his theory as a dialogue theology.[14]

---

12   'İnsanlığın geleceği adına bizim gelecek nesillere en büyük armağanımız geçmişten gelen kin ve nefreti toprağa gömmemiz ve kinsiz, nefretsiz bir dünyayı onlara teslim etmemizdir.' [trans: 'For the sake of humanity, our greatest gift to the future generations will be to bury the hatred and animosity of the past and pass on to them a world which is free of hatred and animosity.'] Fethullah Gülen, 'Ikindi Sohbetleri' (Ahmet Kurucan lecture notes, Pennsylvania, 6th December, 2006).

13   Sufism is the 'inner' dimension of Islam. Gülen defines it as the '[P]ath followed by an individual who, having been able to free himself or herself from human vices and weaknesses in order to acquire angelic qualities and conduct pleasing to God, lives in accordance with the requirements of God's knowledge and love, and in the resulting spiritual delight that ensues.' Fethullah Gülen, Key Concepts in the Practice of Sufism Vol. 1 (Somerset, NJ: The Light, 2007), xii.

14   Writing from a perspective deeply influenced by Gülen's thinking, Ahmet Kurucan and Mustafa Kasim Erol provide a very useful idea of what Gülen's dialogue theology looks like in Dialogue in Islam (London: Dialogue Society, 2012).

Gülen considers dialogue to be inherently and instrumentally valuable. It is inherently valuable because it is in accordance with God's will and the character of his creation. We are social beings, intended to interact and learn about one another; the Qur'an states: 'We... made you into races and tribes so that you should get to know one another' (al-Hujurat, 49:13). Through knowing one another we come to know ourselves, which in turn helps us to know our Creator,[15] according to Gülen.[16] Since the diversity of creation manifests the diversity of God's names and attributes, knowledge of God's diverse creation contributes to our awareness of God.

Dialogue is instrumentally valuable for Gülen primarily because through dialogue people can cooperate and build durable solutions to shared problems. Dialogue is thus a means to community building and peace.

Gülen's approach is practice-focused, exemplified in the activities around the globe of the civil society movement he inspires. There is nothing abstract or esoteric about it. Gülen's history of constant interaction with the public and his profound sense of social responsibility keep his thought connected to practical matters and ordinary people. He is, nevertheless, a scholar, rooting his action in theology and making use of a distinctive range of concepts in his talks, articles and books. Let us now consider the underlying teachings and key concepts which are essential to the dialogue activities Gülen encourages.

15   Al-Ajluni, Kashf al-Khafa, 2:262.
16   Fethullah Gülen, Key Concepts in the Practice of Sufism Vol. 1 (Somerset, NJ: The Light, 2007), 147.

A key point to note about Gülen's approach is that it is based on a human-centric discourse.[17] Because Gülen's worldview is God-centric his view on dialogue is human-centric.[18] Gülen believes that human beings are the greatest manifestation of God's names and attributes, that existence as we know it was created for the consciousness of human beings, that humans are God's vicegerents on earth,[19] that our humanity is our most basic commonality and that before God, in terms of being created all creation is equal.[20] This view of human beings brought about through a God-centric understanding of life and creation leads Gülen to believe that human beings should be respected and engaged with first and foremost because of their humanness. Their faith, religion and nationality come second and are irrelevant at this level of understanding. Showing respect to a fellow human being is a reflection of one's respect to God, his or her Creator. Gülen's vision of dialogue is centred on engagement at the level of our common humanity; his approach is thus inclusive and comprehensive.[21] One who truly embodies

---

17   'Diyalog insanlarla insan olma ortak paydası etrafında toplanmaktır.' [trans: 'Dialogue is about humans coming together around their common humanity'.] Fethullah Gülen, 'Ikindi Sohbetleri' (Ahmet Kurucan lecture notes, Pennsylvania, 14th January, 2006).

18   Fethullah Gülen, Toward a Global Civilization of Love & Tolerance, 50.

19   The role of vicegerent involves using God-given capacities to explore Creation, 'us[ing] everything to its purpose, and [being] the representatives of characteristics that belong to [God], such as knowledge, will, and might.' Fethullah Gülen, 'Humanity and its Responsibilities,' Fethullah Gülen website, last updated 14th June 2006, http://en.fgulen.com/love-and-tolerance/270-the-ideal-human/1829-humanity-and-its-responsibilities.

20   Fethullah Gülen, 'Longing for Love', The Fountain, 64 (2008).

21   Fethullah Gülen, Toward a Global Civilization of *Love and Tolerance,* 116-121.

this approach becomes a '*gönül insanı*' ('a person of the heart'), described by Gülen as follows:

> [they] open their hearts to everyone, welcoming them affectionately [...]. Regarding their deeds and attributes, they try to be compatible with everybody, they try to avoid vicious competition with others, [...] they try to show as much respect as possible to the philosophy and ideas that other people adopt. They turn a blind eye to what other people may do wrong. [...] [S]uch people nullify bad behaviour with kindness, not thinking to hurt anybody, even when they have been hurt over and over again.[22]

An important element of Gülen's human-centric discourse is the belief that diversity is intended.[23] [24] Gülen considers that the Qur'an explicitly conceives of religion in the plural, referring to verses such as this: 'Had your Lord willed, all the people on earth would have believed. So can you [O Prophet] compel

---

22   Fethullah Gülen, 'Portrait of People of Heart,' Fethullah Gülen website, last updated 5th July 2007, http://fgulen .org/recent-articles/2234-the-portrait-of-people-of-heart.html.

23   Gülen, Toward a Global Civilization of *Love and Tolerance*, 250.

24   'Herkesin Müslüman olmasını isteme farklı, Allah'ın iradesi farklı. Herkesin Müslüman olması hiçbir zaman olmamış, demek ki İlahi adet bu değil. Bunu görmemezlikten gelmemeli.' [trans: 'Wanting everyone to embrace Islam is one thing, what God wills is another thing. In the whole of history, never has the whole of mankind embraced Islam. This means that this is not God's tradition ('ilahi adet'). We should not overlook this point.'] Fethullah Gülen, 'İkindi Sohbetleri' (Ahmet Kurucan lecture notes, Pennsylvania, 14th June, 2009).

people to believe?' (*Yunus,* 10:99).[25] As already mentioned, the Qur'an connects human diversity to the divine intention that human beings should get to know one another (*al-Hujurat,* 49:13). For Gülen, diversity of race, religion, nation and life-way was intended by God and should be accepted and valued as a route to understanding. Diversity requires us to learn how to live together, which in turn necessitates dialogue. According to Gülen the response to diversity through positive engagement and dialogue is one of the major goals that the divine will has set for humankind.[26]

Gülen explains that the universe, in all its diversity, was created out of love and compassion.[27] As a result, love and compassion are an underlying theme of Gülen's discourse and shape his views on dialogue. He states that love and compassion should be the basis for all our interaction with one another.[28] They are the foundation of the active pursuit of peace and justice. Combined with spiritual awareness and a proper humility based on awareness of one's own impotence and insignificance, they make a person capable of real dialogue. But it is love and compassion which provide the necessary driving force for engagement in dialogue and other valuable social endeavours. Love's role of driving social action is crucial for Gülen, since in his eyes spirituality and spiritual practices fulfil their potential only when expressed

---

25   Other examples from the Qur'an included verses such as: 'Now the truth has come from your Lord: let those who wish to believe in it do so, and let those who wish to reject it do so,' (al-Kahf, 18:29) and 'There is no compulsion in religion' (al-Baqarah, 2:256).

26   Gülen, Toward a Global Civilization of *Love and Tolerance,* 249–50.

27   Gülen, Toward a Global Civilization of Love and Tolerance, 1, 4.

28   Gülen, Toward a Global Civilization of Love and Tolerance, 4.

through action in society.[29]

Gülen's counsel of love and compassion is complemented by his emphasis on humility and being non-judgemental towards others. This strong sense of humility[30] for Gülen is based on the following perspective: since everything is created and sustained through God, everything is dependent upon Him. As a result no one can take credit for any good that they do, as it is and can only be done in a state of dependence upon God. Therefore we must be humble in recognition of this fact whatever we achieve. We cannot judge others according to Gülen since we are all lost but for the mercy of God, and no one has the right to delimit the mercy of God but God Himself. Gülen advises, 'Be a prosecutor towards yourself an advocate for others'.[31] This state of being is conducive to dialogue since it opens people up to one another and avoids the barriers to dialogue created by arrogant and judgemental attitudes.

Humility and being non-judgmental is also very important to achieve what Gülen calls *hoşgörü* (read '*hoshgoru*'), that is, empathic acceptance.[32] Gülen repeatedly states that dialogue is about empathic acceptance, that is accepting people as they are

29   Heon Kim and John Raines, Making Peace, in and with the World: the Gülen Movement and Eco-Justice (Newcastle upon Tyne: Cambridge Scholars, 2012), 59.

30   Fethullah Gülen, 'Kriterler,' Sızıntı 226 (November, 1997).

31   Fethullah Gülen, 'Kriterler,' Sızıntı 226 (November, 1997).

32   David Capes, 'Tolerance in the Theology and Thought of A J Conyers and F Gülen,' in Muslim World in Transition: Contributions of the Gülen Movement: Conference Proceedings, ed. Ihsan Yilmaz et al (London: Leeds Metropolitan University Press, 2007), 429.

in their own right without judging or trying to change them, let alone convert them.[33] Empathic acceptance requires you to put yourself in the other's position. It puts the other at ease, allowing him to feel comfortable being himself around you, feeling that you appreciate him. Gülen says, 'there should be a chair for everyone within your heart'.[34]

Empathic acceptance is very useful in getting to know one another. When our engagement reaches a deeper level, though, how can we reconcile our own convictions with a readiness to support, learn from and borrow from the other? Regarding this point, Gülen expands on Said Nursi's engagement discourse.[35] He suggests that we should break things down into their basic components such as actions and attributes and respond to these components individually, rather than judging the whole according to a particular part. In the case of another human being, we must love and respect him or her for the sake of his or her humanness. If we dislike something that a person does, we must limit our dislike to the attribute from which that action originates. For example, we should dislike the attribute

---

33   Fethullah Gülen, Fasıldan Fasıla 2 (İzmir: Nil Yayınları, 1996), 155-156.

34   Fethullah Gülen, 'Vicdan Genişliği ve Gerçek Şefkat,' Herkul website, 25th October, 2009, accessed 4th March, 2013, http://www.herkul.org/index.php/bamteli/bamteli-arsiv/7478-Vicdan%20Geni%C5%9Fli%C4%9Fi%20ve%20Ger%C3%A7ek%20%C5%9Eefkat.

35   Said Nursi, Emirdağ Lahikâsı (İstanbul: Söz Basım Yayın, 2004), 2, letter no. 151.

of untruthfulness rather than the untruthful person.[36] The same principle applies when engaging with another culture or civilisation. We should not disregard a culture or civilisation due to certain qualities associated with it, but find ways of embracing the whole while maintaining reservations about those qualities. This approach provides a framework for dialogue at a deeper level in which participants engage openly without necessarily condoning one another's every attribute. It is a framework which may give dialogue participants confidence to engage wholeheartedly and borrow from one another without fear of having to compromise their own beliefs.[37]

Positive action (*müsbet hareket*)[38] is another important emphasis

---

36   'Bizim inancımıza göre insan takdis edilecek varlıktır. Bizim tavrımız, temerrüde, tecavüze, zulme, bağye karşıdır. Yani vasıflaradır.' [trans: 'According to our belief, the human being is a blessed form of creation deserving of utmost respect. Our reaction is towards deception/aggression, violence, oppression and tyranny. In other words, our reaction is towards attributes [of people, not people themselves.'] Fethullah Gülen, 'Ikindi Sohbetleri' (Ahmet Kurucan lecture notes, Pennsylvania, 4th June, 2009).

37   'Evet; bir alış-veriş bu. Başka insanlar, gruplar, kültürler ve medeniyetlerde istifade edilecek değerler vardır; onları alıyoruz. Bizim de istifade edilecek değerlerimiz varsa, onları da veriyoruz.' [trans: 'Yes, this is a give and take. There are values we can benefit from in other people, groups, cultures and civilisations; these we take. If we have any values that are worth benefitting from, these we share.'] Fethullah Gülen, 'Ikindi Sohbetleri' (Ahmet Kurucan lecture notes, Pennsylvania, 1st May, 2009).

38   Fethullah Gülen, 'Müspet Hareketin Ölçüsü,' Fethullah Gülen Turkish website, 15th June, 2007, accessed 1st March, 2013, http://tr.fgulen.com/content/view/13920/3/.

of Gülen's[39] which is very relevant to dialogue. The first point about positive action is that it implies and assumes action. Gülen has an acute sense of our responsibility towards God and towards all of his creation. For him, this responsibility requires conscious effort and action. 'Positive' action, for Gülen, is proactive, not formulated in reaction to someone else's action or position.[40] Reacting to others, allowing them to determine your mode of action, is an uninspiring approach and indicative of a lack of belief in your own goals and methods. Positive action helps people to maintain a positive mind-set, whereas a reactive approach may incline them to perpetuate ongoing disputes and polemics. It involves a level-headedness, a calm, collected, consistent approach.

Positive action requires positive thinking about others (*hüsnüzan*) as opposed to seeing people in a negative light (*suizan*). Gülen points out that when we see others in this light, assuming the worst of them, we nurture a suspicious attitude towards them and a sense of superiority in ourselves.[41] *Suizan* destroys trust and goodwill and is incompatible with dialogue. *Hüsnüzan* as a key concept in *tasawwuf* and in Gülen's philosophy has two interconnected meanings; it can both signify thinking positively

---

39   'Müspet Bütün Hizmetleri Alkışlayalım,' Zaman, 21st February, 2013, accessed 28th February, 2013, http://www.zaman.com.tr/gundem_ muspet-butun-hizmetleri-alkislayalim_2056280.html.

40   Gürkan Çelik, The Gülen Movement: Building Social Cohesion Through Dialogue and Education (Delft: Eburon, 2010), 49.

41   Fethullah Gülen, 'Measure of Selflessness,' Fethullah Gülen website, 16th April 2010, accessed 26th December 2012, http://fgulen.org/recent-articles/3608-measure-of-selflessness.html.

regarding God's designs and decrees,[42] and also thinking well of God's creatures, avoiding negative thoughts and feelings. In this sense, *hüsnüzan* in its comprehensive meaning refers to thinking positively and constructively about others, not taking other people's actions lightly, and avoiding focusing on other people's mistakes.[43] These positive attitudes are at the core of dialogue and proper social conduct in Gülen's thinking.

Having sketched some of the key concepts of Gülen's thinking on dialogue, it is worth noting his emphasis that the inclusivity, depth and range of true dialogue does not by any means imply homogenisation. Gülen is decidedly against dialogue being used to convert people or to create a melting pot in which people lose their distinct identities. He is also against people feeling the need to compromise their faith in order to achieve dialogue.[44] He often counsels people to be themselves in the process of dialogue. If people feel they have to conceal elements of their faith or religious practice or to engage in activities prohibited by their religion, Gülen states that this is no longer dialogue since it contravenes the essential principles of love, compassion, humility and empathic acceptance.

---

42   John Renard, A to Z of Sufism (Plymouth: Scarecrow Press, 2005), 265.

43   Fethullah Gülen 'Başkalarına hüsnüzan nazarıyla bakmak,' Fethullah Gülen Turkish website, 19th December, 2011, accessed 26th December, 2012, http://tr.fgulen.com/content/view/20027/3/.

44   Ahmet Kurucan and Mustafa K. Erol, Dialogue in Islam (London: Dialogue Society, 2012), 20-22.

Dialogue in Practice

Through his teachings and sermons, Fethullah Gülen has inspired a transnational civil society movement engaging in education and dialogue, contributing towards more positive relations between groups of different faiths, cultures and political positions. The movement is faith inspired yet faith neutral in its activities and is increasingly attracting support from people of diverse backgrounds and religions. The movement is loosely connected through shared ideals and teachings, some of which were explored above. In this section, we will consider how Gülen's teachings on dialogue are being put into practice.

Many people involved in or familiar with the movement inspired by Gülen consider that his teachings and advocacy have attuned a large mass of people to a dialogical outlook in their general approach to interpersonal and inter-group relations. This is attributed mainly to two reasons. First, Gülen's general exposition of Islam has always been very inclusive, loving and peaceful, inherently dialogic. Ordinary people influenced by his scholarship have thus adopted a dialogic outlook in their faith. The second reason is that Gülen expressly argues that dialogue is too important to be left to dialogue practitioners or dialogue organisations alone.[45] These people and organisations may have a particular specialism and expertise in dialogue but their efforts must be supported through the collective will of wider

---

45   Gülen, Toward a Global Civilization of *Love and Tolerance,* 77.

society and organisations not explicitly focused on dialogue. To achieve this, all people should be dialogically predisposed, that is respectful of diversity, welcoming and ready to engage, and all organisations, whatever their primary purpose, should utilise dialogue in the course of pursuing their main objectives. In accordance with this view, those people and organisations inspired by Gülen, whether schools, universities, clinics, relief charities, business associations or others, share a commitment to a dialogic approach and to bringing about a more humane, loving, caring and peaceful society.

Schools guided by the principles of Gülen's vision have been founded in around 150 countries. In regions affected by ongoing or recent conflict, including Afghanistan, Pakistan, the Philippines, Bosnia-Herzegovina, southeast Turkey and northern Iraq, the schools, which welcome students from diverse backgrounds, play an important role in easing inter-group tensions.[46] This role is noted by Father Thomas Michel SJ with reference to examples such as the Philippine-Turkish School of Tolerance on the southern Philippine Island of Mindanao. He visited the school in 1995, at a time when the area was ravaged by all kinds of inter-community violence. Around half the school's students were Muslim and half Christian. Michel states that the school offered them, 'an excellent education and a more positive way of living and relating to each other.'[47]

---

46   Harun Akyol, 'How to Solve the Kirkuk Problem?' Today's Zaman, 20th April, 2011, accessed 5th March, 2013, http://todayszaman.com/news-241508-how-to-solve-the-kirkuk-problem-by-harun-akyol*.html.

47   Thomas Michel, 'Fethullah Gülen as Educator,' in Turkish Islam and the Secular State: The Gülen Movement, ed. M Hakan Yavuz and John L. Esposito (Syra Cruz: Syra Cruz University Press, 2003), 70.

From the large pool of people and organisations inspired by Gülen, organisations focused specifically on dialogue have emerged alongside educational initiatives. Because the movement is not centrally organised it is not possible to determine the number of Gülen inspired dialogue organisations, but it is safe to assume that there are Gülen inspired dialogue organisations in approximately 150 countries.[48] Gülen is not officially linked to any of them, accept a handful of which he is the honorary chairman, such as the Journalists and Writers Foundation in Istanbul[49], the Rumi Forum[50] in Washington DC and the Intercultural Dialogue Platform[51] in Brussels.

Like these, the Dialogue Society is a Gülen inspired organisation. The Dialogue Society's guiding principles, summarised below, have been inferred from Gülen's teachings and key concepts, which we explored in the previous section. Other Gülen inspired organisations may have arrived at the same or similar approaches given the shared source of inspiration and guidance. Naturally, the list is not exhaustive.

---

48   One of various indicators suggesting this approximate figure is the presence of Gülen inspired schools in this number of countries; in general, since dialogue organisations can be more easily established than schools, it is likely that those inspired by Gülen will have set up a dialogue organisation in a country where they are also able to found a school.

49   This is the first Gülen inspired dialogue organisation, founded in 1994. Journalists and Writers Foundation, accessed 7th March, 2013, http://www.gyv.org.tr/.

50   Rumi Forum, accessed 5th March, 2013, http://www.rumiforum.org/about/about-rumi-forum.html.

51   Intercultural Dialogue Platform, accessed 5th March, 2013, http://www.dialogueplatform.eu/.

1. To formulate dialogue in the most inclusive way possible

2. While founded and led by Muslims, to be an organisation serving mainstream society

3. To allow dialogue to be dynamic, being open to new developments, forms of engagement and projects

4. To balance dynamism and development with consistency and perseverance

5. To come together around humanness: 'we are human first, then Muslim, Christian, Jew, Hindu or other'

6. To embrace everyone with love, compassion and empathic acceptance: 'there must be a place for everyone in your heart'

7. To insist on peace as the default position: 'however difficult, peace must be sought'

8. To recognise that dialogue is inherently as well as instrumentally valuable

9. To be mindful that dialogue is a natural human expression and that diversity is an intended phenomenon

10. To ensure that dialogue and its activities are positive and proactive and focused on developing greater understanding and trust

11. To focus on core social issues, developing a stronger sense of belonging and concern for one another

12. To be locally driven and motivated, working towards facilitating dialogue within the society in which the organisation is based.

Based on such guiding principles, Gülen inspired dialogue charities worldwide undertake tens of thousands of dialogue initiatives and projects each year, trying to reach out to the disengaged. These charities organise events at various levels, targeting the grass roots of society as well as academics, journalists, policy-makers and community leaders. The Dialogue Society aims to advance social cohesion by connecting communities, empowering people to engage and contributing to the development of ideas on dialogue and community building. It brings people together through discussion forums, courses, capacity building publications and outreach. It operates nation-wide with regional branches across the UK. Through a Master's Degree in Dialogue Studies,[52] the launch of a Journal of Dialogue Studies,[53] a Dialogue School[54] and this very book on dialogue theories it aims amongst other things to contribute towards establishing 'dialogue' as a distinct academic field. It is hoped that the development of such a field will build further momentum for the development of dialogic approaches and initiatives.

---

52   The MA in Dialogue Studies was developed and is delivered in partnership with Keele University. 'Dialogue Studies MA,' Dialogue Society, accessed 5th March, 2013, http://www.dialoguesociety.org/courses/dialogue-studies-ma. html.

53   'Journal of Dialogue Studies,' Dialogue Society, accessed 5th March, 2013, http://www.dialoguesociety.org/publications/academia/829-journal-of-dialogue-studies.html.

54   'Dialogue School', Dialogue Society, accessed 5th March, 2013, http://www.dialoguesociety.org/courses/dialogue-school.html.

Questions for Reflection

1. Gülen's teachings have had an immense impact, not only in Turkey but also internationally. What makes him so influential?

2. Are there any limits to the practice of *hüsnüzan*, in the sense of thinking the best of others? Can *hüsnüzan* be practised sincerely and consistently without naivety?

3. How does one become a 'person of the heart' (gönül insanı)?

4. Gülen's description of dialogue includes different types of activities and conversations that bring people together and result in greater understanding. He states that lasting dialogue will only be achieved if it includes and rests on the grass roots of society. How can dialogue (as defined by Gülen) be extended to include grass roots of society?

5. Are there any limits to 'positive action' and 'empathic acceptance' (musbet hareket and hoşgörü)? If so, what are they?

6. While volunteers of the Hizmet movement seek to promote an inclusive dialogue between diverse groups, the majority of them are inspired by and rooted in the same Islamic faith. What advantages and disadvantages might be associated with this fact?

Bibliography

Akyol, Harun. 'How to Solve the Kirkuk Problem?' *Today's Zaman*, 20 April, 2011. Accessed 5th March, 2013. http://todayszaman.com/news-241508-how-to-solve-the-kirkuk-problem-by-harun-akyol*.html.

Cantori, Louis J. 'Fethullah Gülen: Kemalist and Islamic Republicanism and the Turkish Democratic Future.' In *Muslim World in Transition: Contributions of the Gülen Movement: Conference Proceedings,* edited by Ihsan Yilmaz et al., 77-103. London: Leeds Metropolitan University Press, 2007.

Capes, David. 'Tolerance in the Theology and Thought of A J Conyers and F Gülen.' In *Muslim World in Transition: Contributions of the Gülen Movement: Conference Proceedings*, edited by Ihsan Yilmaz et al., 428-429. London: Leeds Metropolitan University Press, 2007.

Çelik, Gurkan. *The Gülen Movement: Building Social Cohesion through Dialogue and Education*. Nieuwegein: Eburon, 2010.

Dialogue Society. Accessed 25th March, 2013. www.dialoguesociety.org.

Fethullah Gülen Turkish website. 'Başkalarına hüsnüzan nazarıyla bakmak.' Accessed 26th December, 2012. http://tr.fgulen.com/content/view/20027/3/

Gülen, Fethullah. *Criteria or Lights on the Way*, 2nd ed. Izmir: Kaynak, 1998.

Gülen, Fethullah. *Fasıldan Fasıla* 2. Izmir: Nil Yayınları, 1996.

Gülen, Fethullah. 'Humanity and its Responsibilities.' Fethullah Gülen website. Last updated 14th June 2006. http://en.fgulen. com/love-and-tolerance/270-the-ideal-human/1829-humanity-and-its-responsibilities.

Gülen, Fethullah. *Key Concepts in the Practice of Sufism Vol. 1.* Somerset, NJ: The Light, 2007.

Gülen, Fethullah. 'Kriterler.' *Sızıntı* 226 (November 1997).

Gülen, Fethullah. 'Measure of Selflessness.' Fethullah Gülen website, 16th April 2010. Accessed 26th December, 2012. http://www.fethullahgulen.org/gulens-works/296-recent-articles/3608-measure-of-selflessness.html.

Gülen, Fethullah. 'Müspet Hareketin Ölçüsü.' Fethullah Gülen Turkish website, 15th June, 2007. Accessed 1st March, 2013. http://tr.fgulen.com/content/view/13920/3/.

Gülen, Fethullah. 'Portrait of People of Heart.' Fethullah Gülen website. Last updated 5th July 2007. http://fgulen.org/recent-articles/2234-the-portrait-of-people-of-heart.html.

Gülen, Fethullah. 'Science and Religion.' In *Knowledge and Responsibility: Islamic Perspectives on Science*, edited by Ali Ünal. Somerset, NJ: Tughra Books, 2007.

Gülen, Fethullah. *Toward a Global Civilization of Love & Tolerance.* Somerset, NJ: Light, Inc, 2006.

Gülen, Fethullah. 'Vicdan Genişliği ve Gerçek Şefkat.' Herkul website, 25th October, 2009. Accessed 4th March, 2013. http://www.herkul.org/index.php/bamteli/bamteli-arsiv/7478-Vicdan%20Geni%C5%9Fli%C4%9Fi%20 ve%20Ger%C3%A7ek%20%C5%9Eefkat.

Hunt, Robert A. and Yuksel A. Aslandogan. *Muslim Citizens of the Globalized World: Contributions of the Gülen Movement.* Somerset, NJ: The Light, 2007.

Intercultural Dialogue Platform. Accessed 5th March, 2013.
http://www.dialogueplatform.eu/.
Journalists and Writers Foundation. Accessed 7th March, 2013.
http://www.gyv.org.tr/.
Kim, Heon and John Raines. *Making Peace, in and with the
World: the Gülen Movement and Eco-Justice.* New Castle upon
Tyne: Cambridge Scholars, 2011.
Kurucan, Ahmet and Mustafa Kasim Erol. *Dialogue in Islam.*
London: Dialogue Society, 2012.
Michel, Thomas. 'Fethullah Gülen as Educator.' In *Turkish
Islam and the Secular State: The Gülen Movement,* edited by M
Hakan Yavuz and John L. Esposito, 67-82. Syra Cruz: Syra
Cruz University Press, 2003.
Nursi, Said. *Emirdağ Lahikâsı.* Istanbul: Söz Basım Yayın, 2004.
Renard, John. *A to Z of Sufism.* Plymouth: Scarecrow Press, 2005.
Rumi Forum. Accessed 5th March, 2013. http://www.rumiforum.
org/about/about-rumi-forum.html.
Ünal, Ali ed. *Knowledge and Responsibility: Islamic Perspectives on
Science.* Somerset, NJ: Tughra Books, 2007.
Yilmaz, Ihsan, Eileen Barker, Henri J. Barkey, Muhammad
Abdul Haleem, George S. Harris, Thomas Michel, Simon
Robinson, Zeki Saritoprak, David Thomas, Paul Weller, Ian
G. Williams, Alan Godlas, Asaf Hussain, Johnston McMaster,
Colin Turner and Tim Winter, eds. *Muslim World in Transition:
Contributions of the Gülen Movement: Conference Proceedings.*
London: Leeds Metropolitan University Press, 2007.
Zaman. 'Müspet Bütün Hizmetleri Alkışlayalım.' *Zaman,*
21st February, 2013. Accessed 28th February, 2013. http://
www.zaman.com.tr/gundem_muspet-butun-hizmetleri-
alkislayalim_2056280.html.

Recommended Reading

Gülen's Works:

Gülen, Fethullah. *Criteria or Lights on the Way,* 2nd ed. Izmir: Kaynak, 1998.

Gülen, Fethullah. *Key Concepts in the Practice of Sufism Vol. 1.* Somerset, NJ: The Light, Inc., 2007.

Gülen, Fethullah. *Key Concepts in the Practice of Sufism Vol 2.* Somerset, NJ: The Light, Inc., 2004.

Gülen, Fethullah. *Key Concepts in the Practice of Sufism Vol. 3.* Clifton, NJ: Tughra Books, 2009.

Gülen, Fethullah. *Key Concepts in the Practice of Sufism Vol. 4.* Clifton, NJ: Tughra Books, 2010.

Gülen, Fethullah. *Toward a Global Civilization of Love & Tolerance.* Somerset, NJ: Light, Inc, 2006.

Commentary:

Barton, Greg, Paul Weller and Ihsan Yilmaz eds. *The Muslim World and Politics in Transition: Creative Contributions of the Gülen Movement.* London, New Delhi, New York and Sydney: Bloomsbury, 2013.

Hendrick, Joshua D. *Gülen: The Ambiguous Politics of Market Islam in Turkey and the World.* New York and London: New York University Press, 2013.

Turam, Berna. *Between Islam and the State: The Politics of Engagement.* Stanford, California: Stanford University Press, 2007.

Weller, Paul, and Ihsan Yılmaz. *European Muslims, Civility and*

Public Life: Perspectives on and from the Gülen Movement. London: Continuum, 2012.

Yavuz, Hakan. *Toward an Islamic Enlightenment: The Gülen Movement.* New York, NY: Oxford University Press, 2013.

Yilmaz, Ihsan, Eileen Barker, Henri J. Barkey, Muhammad Abdul Haleem, George S. Harris, Thomas Michel, Simon Robinson, Zeki Saritoprak, David Thomas, Paul Weller, Ian G. Williams, Alan Godlas, Asaf Hussain, Johnston McMaster, Colin Turner and Tim Winter, eds. *Muslim World in Transition: Contributions of the Gülen Movement: Conference Proceedings.* London: Leeds Metropolitan University Press, 2007.

Practical Applications:

Çelik, Gurkan. *The Gülen Movement: Building Social Cohesion through Dialogue and Education.* Nieuwegein: Eburon, 2010.

Cetin, Muhammed. *Gülen Movement: Civic Service without Borders.* New York, NY: Blue Dome Press, 2010.

Dialogue Society. Accessed 25th March, 2013. www.dialoguesociety.org.

Hunt, Robert A., and Yuksel A. Aslandogan. *Muslim Citizens of the Globalized World: Contributions of the Gülen Movement.* Somerset, NJ: The Light, 2007.

Journalists and Writers Foundation. Accessed 7th March, 2013. http://www.gyv.org.tr/

Kim, Heon and John Raines. *Making Peace, in and with the World: the Gülen Movement and Eco-Justice.* New Castle upon Tyne: Cambridge Scholars, 2011.

Yilmaz, Ihsan et al. eds. *Muslim World in Transition: Contributions of the Gülen Movement: Conference Proceedings.* London: Leeds Metropolitan University Press, 2007.